## How relevant is this book?

It answers most every question a golfer will ever be confronted with - in seconds.

It clearly resolve
when relief is po
rules infringemen

GW00361175

It should be carri
rules official.

## What makes it spec

The rules of golf apply differently when a ball is on the fairway to when in a bunker, or water hazard, or other designated course area. This book dissects the course and shows what rules apply when a ball is in a particular part of the course.

## Don't the official rules do this?

No; and other books that have been based on the "Do I Get A Drop?" format, are not nearly as comprehensive or user friendly, and are more expensive.

## The easy way to find golf rules answers

# The "DO I GET A DROP?" Family

The books that every golfer needs

## OTHER SUBJECTS

Author:

Douglas Anderson

## What is a valid stroke?

A forward movement of the club at the players own ball made with the intention of hitting and moving the ball; but not including any swing voluntarily aborted. The backswing is not part of a valid stroke. Any infringements incurred in the backswing such as moving loose impediments in hazards, result in a penalty - 2 strokes. Strokes made other than "as defined" are not counted. An unintentional hit such as during a practice swing (at a ball in play) is not a valid stroke, nor is a swipe in anger. In both cases the stroke is not counted, but a 1 stroke penalty is incurred and the ball is replaced.

The manner of striking the ball is also regulated. The ball must not be pushed or scooped and must be struck at with the head of the club (either front, back or side). The penalty for infringing the striking regulations is 2 strokes.

The order of play from the first tee is as called by the starter. Should start of play be not under starters control, the order of play would be determined by casting lots (flip a coin).

## Ball falls from tee (moving ball)
Swing aborted      - no penalty - re tee
Swing completed      - no penalty but
     count 1 stroke for completed swing - ball is in
     play and cannot be re-teed without penalty

## Hitting from wrong teeing area
(Swing is not counted - stroke must be replayed)
     In front of markers      - penalty 2 strokes
     Outside of markers      - penalty 2 strokes
     (stance - may be outside - not ball)
     More than two club lengths
         behind markers      - penalty 2 strokes
     Failure to replay from correct area - disqualification

## Practice Swing    - ball (not yet in play)    - no penalty &
                knocked from tee      re-tee free

**THE TEE**

## FAIRW
(closely mown area)

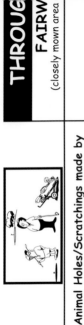

| | FAIRWAY (closely mown area) |
|---|---|
| **Animal Holes/Scratchings made by**<br>- burrowing animals, reptiles & birds<br>- non-burrowing animals | Ball in, or sw |
| **Ball Moved** | |
| **Bare Patches** | |
| **Casual Water**<br><br>- ball found<br>- ball lost in water | For rel<br>taking normal s<br><br>Free drop - |
| **Cleaning Ball** - when taking relief<br>- not in relief situations | |
| **Dirt/Soil/Sand** | Remov |

| | ROUGH (not so closely mown) |
|---|---|
| ...ce interfered by - free drop - 1 club length ∗ (Page 4) | No relief |
| | See page 16 |
| | No relief |
| ...vailable water must be visible before or after ...hy ground provides no relief nor does dew or frost. ...e drop - 1 club length ∗ (Page 4) ...th (relief is from estimated last entry point) ∗ (Page 4) | |
| Permitted - no penalty Penalty 1 stroke | |
| ...ove lie, stance, swing etc - Penalty 2 strokes | |

| Dropping Ball (page 21) ★ | 1 club length drops<br>or if lost, from<br>or obstruction (w<br>**Note:** Relief f<br>and also from immov<br>of some other fac<br>takin |
| --- | --- |
| 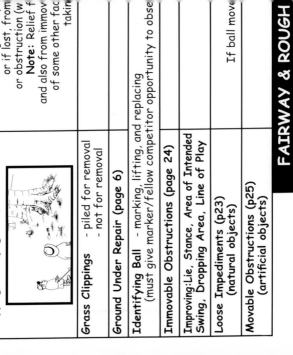 | |
| Grass Clippings   - piled for removal<br>                - not for removal | |
| Ground Under Repair (page 6) | |
| Identifying Ball - marking, lifting, and replacing<br>(must give marker/fellow competitor opportunity to obse | |
| Immovable Obstructions (page 24) | |
| Improving:Lie, Stance, Area of Intended<br>Swing, Dropping Area, Line of Play | |
| Loose Impediments (p23)<br>      (natural objects) | |
| Movable Obstructions (p25)<br>      (artificial objects) | If ball move |

**FAIRWAY & ROUGH**

ured from the nearest point of relief to where the ball lies,
ated point where the ball last entered the abnormal ground
t nearer the hole and is not in a hazard or on a green).
rmal ground, including, animal holes, casual water, G.U.R.
uctions is not permitted if a stroke is not possible because
as a tree or roots or if the interference results only from
rmal stance, swing or direction of play.

ree drop - 1 club length *
e impediment relief (page 23)

ree drop - 1 club length *

mitted - but 1 stroke penalty if done without giving
ortunity to observe or if done when not necessary

ree drop - 1 club length *

Penalty 2 strokes
e page 18 for amplification

Remove - no penalty
ult of removing - penalty 1 stroke and replace ball

Remove - no penalty
oves - no penalty - replace ball

| | |
|---|---|
| Paths & Roads   - soil/clay/dirt<br>   - artificial | |
| Playing Moving Ball | Penalty - 2 st<br>swing commenced |
| Plugged Ball | A free drop at ne<br>hole, but only i<br>bet |
| Sprinkler Heads | Free drop from |
| Staked Trees | |
| Unplayable Ball | |
| Wheel Tracks   - pull carts<br>   - motor carts<br>   - machinery | (most clubs grant |
| Wrong Ball Played   - a ball substituted....<br>   - not your ball.... | (Whether intenti |

**FAIRWAY & ROUGH**

No relief

e drop - 1 club length  * (Page 4)

epting that if ball commenced to move after back
penalty. If you caused the ball to move see page 16
possible "ball moved" penalty.

t of relief is allowed for a ball plugged in its own plug
is on a closely mown part of the course. Grass paths
s will give relief if mown to fairway level.

e drop - 1 club length  * (Page 4)

also from tree if local rule - 1 club length  * (Page 4)

See page 22

No relief
No relief
No relief

machinery tracks under local rules)

t) - Count stroke - play as lies - penalty 2 strokes
t stroke - re-play - penalty 2 strokes
- failure to re-play - disqualification

**FAIRWAY & ROUGH**

5

# GROUND UNDER REPAIR (G.U.R.)

A ball is in G.U.R. when any part is inside or touches the Ground Under Repair.
Anything growing in G.U.R. is part of G.U.R. even if extending beyond boundary.

Ball in, or swing or normal stance interfered by.
**Relief** - Free drop 1 club length from nearest point of relief (which is not nearer the hole, and is not in a hazard or on a green) excepting, that:
  (i) Where making a stroke is not possible because of some other factor such as a tree or roots (outside of the G.U.R. area), or
  (ii) The obstruction only interferes as a result of taking an abnormal stance, swing or direction of play, then . . . free relief is not available.

**Ball lost in designated G.U.R.**
Free drop - relief is from estimated final entry point.
If that point is in a bunker, drop must be in bunker or for 1 stroke penalty outside the bunker keeping drop point and estimated last entry point in line with the flag.

**Ball in designated G.U.R.** - Play as is or free drop.

**Bush or tree in G.U.R.**

Failure to drop outside of designated compulsory G.U.R.
- penalty - 2 strokes

### Grass clippings
Free drop if piled for removal, loose impediment relief if not (page 23)

### G.U.R. not designated
Where ground staff have commenced course maintenance but not marked work area as G.U.R. such as holes dug, timber cut for removal, such areas can be treated as G.U.R. Aeration holes on greens are not work in progress and no relief is available.

### Stakes delineating G.U.R.
Can be either movable or immovable obstructions depending on how solidly embedded. Easily moved stakes are often declared immovable obstructions under local rules.

### Wheel tracks
Neither pull cart, motorised cart or machinery tracks are G.U.R. and no relief is available. (Local rules often allow for relief from machinery tracks).

## Animal Holes/Scratchings
- made by
  - burrowing animals, reptiles & birds
  - non-burrowing animals
  - ball in or sw
    - stance inter

## Ball Moves
- when removing movable obstruction
- after stance taken
- in searching for ball

## Casual Water
- ball lost in or ball retrievable

## Dropping Ball (page 21)
* 1 club length drops are meas
  to where the ball lies, not nec
  the bunker, then (n.p.o.r.) fr

## Grassy Islands in Bunker

| mal | - free drop (in bunker) - 1 club length * | - no penalty<br>- no relief |
|---|---|---|
| | - no penalty - replace ball<br>- penalty 1 stroke - replace ball<br>- no penalty - replace ball | |
| | - free drop (in bunker) 1 club length *<br>- if full relief not available, drop in place of least water, or for 1 stroke penalty drop<br>(1) behind bunker, keeping spot where ball lay in a straight line between drop point and the hole, or<br>(2) from where previous shot was played. | |
| | from the nearest point of relief (within the bunker)<br>he hole. If the ball is lost in casual water within<br>he estimated point where the ball last entered the water. | |
| | - are not part of bunker. Ball can be played where lies, or relief taken under unplayable ball options (page 22) | |

**BUNKER**

7

| Grounding Club or touching ground or loose impediments with the hand or club | - searching for ball<br>- other (when ball is in hazard excepting, that where the lie of been tested, grounding a club<br>  - removing movable obstruct<br>  - to prevent falling<br>  - measuring, picking up or pla<br>  - smoothing sand or soil after fa |
|---|---|

**Identifying Ball** - marking, lifting, and replacing
(must give marker/fellow competitor opportunity to obser

**Immovable Obstructions (page 24)**

**Loose Impediments (natural objects) page 23** - to move or remo
  - in searching for ball

    - in back swing
    - other accidental

  - other

**Movable Obstructions (artificial objects) page 25**

**BUNKER**

hing with the hand in the following situations incurs no penalty:

is not improved, nor the hazard condition deemed to have

xit (provided swing area, stance or line of play are not improved)

(where permitted)

- no penalty
- penalty 2 strokes

- free drop - (in bunker) 1 club length * (Page 7) or for 1 stroke penalty outside the bunker keeping drop point and where ball lay in line with the flag.

- permitted - but 1 stroke penalty if done without giving opportunity to observe or if done when not necessary

- no penalty and replace impediment (small part of ball may be left exposed)
- penalty 2 strokes
- no penalty unless lie or area of intended swing or stance improved.
- penalty 2 strokes

- remove - no penalty

Playing Moving Ball

Plugged Ball
- in bunker
- in grass outside

Rake outside bunker stopping ball from rolling into bunker

Raking prior to playing stroke
- searching for ball
- otherwise

Searching for Ball - probing, touching, raking

Stones

Unplayable Ball

Wrong Ball Played
- a ball substituted
- not your ball

(Whether intentio

**BUNKER**

- penalty - 2 strokes excepting that if ball commenced to move after back swing started there is no penalty. If you caused the ball to move see page 16 for possible "ball moved" penalty.

- no relief
- free relief only if on the closely mown area

- remove rake and if ball rolls, place in original position, or in nearest spot outside the bunker where ball will rest - no penalty

- no penalty
- penalty - 2 strokes

- no penalty - ball must be restored to original position (small part of ball may be left exposed).

- removable only if authorised by local rule

- refer to page 22

ot) - Count stroke - play as lies - penalty 2 strokes
nt stroke - re-play - penalty 2 strokes
     - failure to re-play - disqualification

**BUNKER**

9

# WATE

Water hazards are delineated by yellow posts and
 inside the margin of the hazard. Sta

*Options* - Play as lie

The relief options from red posted areas (calle
from yellow posted hazards. The principal optio

(1) Drop ball behind hazard (no limit on dista
 hazard between the drop point and the fl
(2) Play from where previous shot was played

*For red posted hazards the additional optio*

(3) The point where the ball last entered the haz
(4) A point on the opposite side of the hazar
 was last crossed equidistant from the ho

| Animal Holes / Scratchings |
| --- |
| **Assumption** - ball in hazard |
| Ball Fails to exit hazard or enters |
| another water hazard |

...ts. A ball is in a water hazard when any part is
...ining a hazard are obstructions within the hazard.
... located) or for 1 stroke penalty take relief.

...ral hazards) include two more options than
...relief from water hazards are:
...ping point where ball last entered the

...: drop within two club lengths of:

... nearer the hole.
...osite to the point where the hazard

... relief

... must be known or almost certain that ball entered
...azard, else ball must be played as a lost ball

...ay as lies or for penalty (1 stroke) play from where the
...revious stroke was played or choose from the options
...available when the ball first entered the hazard.

| Ball Lost in Water Hazard | |
|---|---|
| **Ball Moves** | - when removing movable obstruction<br>- after stance taken<br>- in searching for ball |

| Bridge Over Hazard | |
|---|---|
| **Casual Water** | |

| ***Grounding Club* or touching ground, water or loose impediments with the hand or club** | - searching for ball<br>- other (when ball is in hazard excepting, that where the lie of been tested, grounding a clu<br>  - to prevent falling<br>  - removing movable obstruct<br>  - measuring, picking up or pla<br>  - smoothing sand or soil after fo |

| **Identifying Ball**    - marking, lifting, and replacing<br>(must give marker/fellow competitor opportunity to obse | |

| **Immovable Obstructions (page 24)** | |

**WATER HAZARD**

ame options as ball in water hazard

o penalty - replace ball
enalty 1 stroke - replace ball
o penalty - replace ball

s in hazard but can ground club without penalty

o relief from any water in a water hazard

o penalty
enalty 2 strokes
l is not improved, nor the hazard condition deemed to have
ching with the hand in the following situations incurs no penalty:

ll (where permitted)
exit (provided swing area, stance or line of play are not improved)

ermitted - but 1 stroke penalty if done without giving
opportunity to observe or if done when not necessary

o relief

**Loose Impediments (natural objects) page 23** - to move or rem
- in searching for ball

- in back swing
- other accidental

- other

**Movable Obstructions (artificial objects) page 25**

**Playing Moving Ball** - no penalty to hit while moving in water unl

**Plugged Ball**

**Stake Missing - Ball Clearly in Hazard**

**Stakes Delineating Hazard** - easily removable
- not easily removable

**Unplayable Ball**

**Unsure if Ball in Hazard**

**Water overflows hazard posts** - beyond posts is casual water

**Wheel Tracks**

**Wrong Ball Played** - a ball substituted.... (Whether intentionally
- not your ball.... Don't count stroke - re-play
Note: playing a ball moving in wat

# WATER HAZARD

o penalty and replace impediment
small part of ball may be left exposed)
enalty 2 strokes
o penalty unless lie or area of intended
wing or stance improved
enalty 2 strokes

emove - no penalty
ot was delayed for current or wind to improve position.
o relief

all is considered to be in hazard
emove unless declared immovable by local rule
o relief if ball is in hazard
all in water hazard cannot be declared unplayable

must be played as lost ball
ree drop, 1 club length nearest point of relief, not nearer the hole
o relief
t) - Count stroke - play as lies - penalty 2 strokes
enalty 2 strokes - failure to re-play - disqualification
at is in fact a wrong ball, incurs no cost

**WATER HAZARD** 12

# THE GREEN

**A ball is holed when it is at rest in t**

| | |
|---|---|
| **Animal Holes/Scratchings**<br>- made by burrowing animals reptiles & birds | - ball in, or stroke or normal sta<br>  interfered by |
| **Ball Interfering With or<br>Assisting Any Player** | - such ball(s) must be marke<br>- failure to do so when reque |
| **Ball Marker Accidentally Moved** | - marking or replacing b<br>- other |
| **Ball Moves**<br>(also see p16) | - while marking or replacing t<br>  removing loose impediment<br>  old holes or ball pitch mar<br>- before ball addressed<br>- after ball addressed |
| **Ball Overhangs Hole** | - drops more than 10 secon<br>  reaches hole (without un |
| **Ball Played from Off Green** | - strikes another ball (fr<br>- deflected by outside agen<br>- picked-up by outside agen<br>  animal, human or equipmen<br>  (other than the players) |

(A ball is on the green when any part is on)

ole and fully below the top thereof.

| | |
|---|---|
| line of putt | - free place - nearest point of relief not nearer the hole & not in a hazard |
| uested | - penalty 2 strokes |
| suring, moving a loose impediment - no penalty - replace marker | - penalty 1 stroke |
| removing marker, or measuring, vable obstructions, or repairing | - no penalty - replace ball<br>- no penalty - play as lies<br>- penalty - 1 stroke - replace ball |
| er player y) | - add 1 stroke |
| e group) | - no penalty - play where lies<br>- no penalty - play where lies<br>- place where picked-up<br>(substitute ball if necessary - no penalty) |

**THE GREEN**

| | |
|---|---|
| **Ball Played From On Green** | - strikes another ball (from s... |
| | - deflected by outside agenc... |
| | - picked-up by outside agenc... |
| **Ball Strikes Flag Stick** - if resting on flag - remove flag - if t... | |
| - played from off green - flag unattend... | |
| - if attended | |
| - played from on green | |
| **Casual Water** | - free placing - nearest poin... |
| | nearest relief is off the gr... |
| **Cleaning Ball** | - by rubbing on green |
| | |
| **Dropping** | - ball is only dropped on gre... |
| | penalty relief options. In... |
| **Growing Things** | - removing without local rule... |
| **Immovable Obstructions (p24)** | - relief - at nearest point |
| **Line Of Putt** - standing on - intentionally | |
| - accidentally, inadvertently, or to av... | |
| - mopping up dew, frost or water | |

**THE GREEN**

| | |
|---|---|
| up) | - penalty 2 strokes if ball moves |
| e 13) | - no penalty if ball does not move |
| e 13) | - replay |
| | - replay - (substitute ball if necessary) |
| ps it is holed | - no penalty |
| | - penalty 2 strokes |
| | - penalty 2 strokes |
| ef (which is not nearer the hole or in a hazard). If n that is where the ball is placed. | - no penalty unless deliberately testing green |
| er "unplayable ball" and "lateral water hazard" er situations it must be placed. | |
| | - penalty - 2 strokes |
| ef (not nearer the hole or in a hazard) - free place | |
| | - penalty - 2 strokes |
| nding on another players line of putt | - no penalty |
| | - penalty - 2 strokes |

| | |
|---|---|
| **Loose Impediments (p23)** and **Movable Obstructions (p25)** | - remove before stroke<br>- remove while ball in motion |
| **Marking and Replacing Ball** | - marking - allowed by anyone authorised<br>- replacement - must be by the player or pers<br>- by anyone else - if not correcte |
| **Order of Play** | - furthest from hole.<br>A player nearer the hole |
| **Pitch Marks / Old Holes** | - repair |
| **Playing while a putt is in motion** | - when not your turn |
| **Playing Moving Ball** | |
| **Spike Marks** | - to flatten spike marks i |
| **Testing Surface** | - intentional testing by rolli<br>rubbing the green |
| **Wrong Ball Played** | - a ball substituted.... (Whether intentio<br>- not your ball.... D |

| | |
|---|---|
| id contact | - no penalty<br>- penalty - 2 strokes - exceptions - attended flag, flag on ground, & players equipment. |
| player<br>marked ball | - penalty - 1 stroke |
| uested to mark | - etiquette matter<br>can putt instead |
| | - no penalty |
| | - penalty 2 strokes |
| | - penalty - 2 strokes excepting that if ball commenced to move after back swing started there is no penalty. If you caused the ball to move see page 16 for possible "ball moved" penalty. |
| vers line of play | - penalty - 2 strokes<br>or<br>- penalty - 2 strokes |
| not) - Count stroke - play as lies - penalty 2 strokes<br>nt stroke - re-play - penalty 2 strokes<br>- failure to re-play - disqualification | |

# ANYWHERE

| | |
|---|---|
| **Advice** | - asking for or giving advice other than common knowle |
| **Assistance** | - accepting assistance while playing a shot such<br>weather, indicating line of putt etc. |
| **Ball deflected by outside agency** | (animal, human or equipm<br>- played from off green |

**Ball Moved but returns to original spot**

**Ball Moved but doesn't return**
- moved by another ball, or an outside agency (animal, hu
- moved or caused to be moved by the player (or play
- accidentally in:
  - marking or replacing ball, or measuring
  - searching in hazard, g.u.r. or other abnor
  - casual water, or in or on an obstruction.
  - practice swing (when ball is "in play")
  - removing loose impediments (when not
  - removing movable obstructions
  - \* - picking up or touching other than where permi
  - other than above

**Ball Played From Wrong Spot**
- no significant advantage obtained - play as lies
- significant advantage obtained - if not replayed

| | |
|---|---|
| **Ball rolls** | - before ball addressed (not grounded club - or in haz<br>- after ball addressed |

| | |
|---|---|
| distance | - penalty 2 strokes |
| tection from | - penalty 2 strokes |
| her than the players) | - play as lies |
| equipment - other than the players) - replace ball ipment) | - no penalty excepting * |
| und such as | - no penalty - replace ball |
| en) | - no penalty - replace ball |
| the rules * | - penalty 1 stroke - replace ball<br>- penalty 1 stroke - replace ball<br>- penalty 1 stroke<br>- no penalty - replace ball<br>- penalty 1 stroke<br>- penalty 1 stroke - replace ball<br>- penalty 2 strokes (inclusive of any associated "ball moved" penalty)<br>- disqualification |
| en stance) | - no penalty - play as lies<br>- penalty 1 stroke - replace ball |

| | |
|---|---|
| **Ball Strikes Other Players person or Equipment** | (Played fr |
| **Ball Strikes the Player or Player's Equipment** | |
| **Ball taken by outside agency** (animal or human) | |
| | - Ball in motion - played from off green |
| | - played from on green |
| | - Ball stationary |
| **Ball Unfit for Play** - ball may be marked, lifted, examined (not clean | |
| | replaced - (if unfit for use) |
| **Clubs** - borrowing from other players or carrying more than 14 or | |
| | - using club damaged through normal use |
| | - using club damaged through misuse |
| | - applying tape/gauze to assist gripping the club |
| | - using towel or handkerchief to help grip |
| **Discontinuing Play** | - bad weather |
| (without committee authorisation) | - lightning/emergencies |
| **Double or Multiple Hits** | - count stroke and |
| **Equity** - if no rule covers a situation then what would be fair un | |
| | the circumstances should apply. eg. to avoid wildlife |
| **Exerting Influence on Ball Including:** | - picking up loose impedime |
| | or a ball in play to avoi |

**ANYWHERE**

| | |
|---|---|
| green) | - no penalty - play as lies |
| | - penalty 1 stroke - play as lies |
| | - replace where taken<br>- replay<br>- replace where taken |
| | - with scorers consent - no penalty<br>- without scorers consent - penalty 1 stroke |
| -conforming clubs | - penalty 2 strokes per hole (max 4 str.)<br>- no penalty<br>- disqualification<br>- disqualification<br>- no penalty |
| | - disqualification<br>- committee may approve |
| | - penalty 1 stroke |
| | - free drop |
| able obstructions in motion | - penalty 2 strokes - exceptions - attended flag, flag on ground, and players' equipment. (A ball in play or its marker/coin is not "equipment".) |

**ANYWHERE**

**Improving Lie, Stance, Area of Intended Swing, Dropping Ar...**
- in "fairly" taking stance, making stroke (forward movement), backs...
  - otherwise, including:
- removing sand, soil, immovable obstructions, casual water, d...
- bending or breaking grass, flowers, twigs, branches
- leveling or pressing down sand soil divots spike marks or buil...
- shaking water from bushes, trees

**Line of Sight** - immovable obstruction inhibiting vision

**Lost Ball** - in G.U.R. or movable or immovable obstruction
- other - search time - 5 minutes from player/caddy commencing se...
  ball in play until 5 minutes elapses or the ball is replaced; i.e. anot...
  the ball is on a tee, a stroke made. Time playing a wrong ball is exclu...
- a ball located after 5 minutes becomes a wrong ball if playe...
- failure to rectify

**Marking Ball** - if requested by a player, ball must be marked e...
  (If lie is interfered with by a players stroke, it...

**Order of Play** - furthest from hole - regardless of whether...

**Practice Chipping & Putting** (during course round - not holding...
- on green completed, teeing area of next hole
- other than above

**Waiving Rules** - agreeing to do so including failure to apply kno...

**Wrong Green** - ball must be dropped off green - 1 club length (p...

**ANYWHERE**

| ine of Play | completed stroke (when not in a hazard) - no penalty |
|---|---|
| | - penalty 2 strokes, excepting, that on the green, sand and soil can be removed and pitch marks and old holes repaired, and on the tee making or removing ground irregularities is permitted. |
| + | |
| nce | |
| | - no relief (unless by local rule) |
| ball remains the dropped, or if | - free relief, see p6, p25 or p24<br>- penalty 1 stroke and replay from where previous stroke played. If lost in a water hazard other options available (p11)<br>- penalty 2 strokes<br>- disqualification |
| hazards (estored) | - failure to so do - penalty 2 strokes |
| n or not | - etiquette matter |
| tice area | - no penalty ( unless by local rule)<br>- penalty 2 strokes |
| enalty | - disqualification |
| enalty | - penalty 2 strokes if played from green |

**ANYWHERE**

18

A ball is out of bounds when all of the ball is beyond the course side of an out of bounds fence or otherwise designated boundary (at ground level).

When a ball is hit Out Of Bounds, the shot must be replayed by dropping a ball as near as possible to where the previous shot was played - penalty 1 stroke

The Out Of Bounds fence or posts are in fact Out Of Bounds, and no free relief is available from them.

Any ladder etc. on the course side of the fence is an immovable obstruction and relief is available - see page 24.

A ball that is not Out Of Bounds may be played from a stance Out Of Bounds.

# PROVISIONAL BALL

**When to play:** *A provisional ball may be played, if it is considered that the ball played* may *be out of bounds or* may *be lost outside of a water hazard.*

**When not to play:** *A provisional ball cannot be played if:*
  (1)  The ball played is definitely in a water hazard, or
  (2)  The player has gone forward to search for the ball.

It is not possible to "go back" to play a provisional ball. Any ball played in such circumstances becomes the ball in play regardless of the status of the previous ball. The point at which the original ball becomes "out of play" is when another ball is dropped or if on a tee is struck at, or the five minute search time has elapsed.

If a provisional ball is played, and it is subsequently determined that the original ball *was* lost in a water hazard, there are no repercussions. The original ball is in play under the water hazard rules and the provisional ball is picked up without cost.

Where a provisional ball has been played, it may be hit as a provisional ball until the anticipated position of the original ball is reached. If the original ball is then found, it is the ball in play, whether desired or not, and the provisional ball ceases to exist (with no cost). If it is not found, the provisional ball is the ball in play. The penalty for the loss of the original ball, the stroke that caused it to be lost, and the stroke with the provisional ball result in the player recording 3 strokes, for a distance hoped for in 1 stroke.

When first playing a provisional ball, it is essential to advise ones marker that a provisional ball is to be played. Failure to do so results in the ball becoming the ball in play and the original ball being treated as lost.

# DROPPING BALL (relief situations)

**How to Drop.** In all cases, the ball must be dropped (not spun) from an erect stance and with an extended arm at shoulder height. It must strike the ground within the allowable area but may travel for up to a further 2 club lengths (not nearer the hole than the problem point or nearest point of relief) without requiring re-dropping. The ball can therefore finish as much as four club lengths from the problem point.

**Where to Drop.** The circumstances where relief dropping apply are shown on the "Where Are You?" pages. Turn to the page for the part of the course where your ball lies.

**Finding Nearest Point of Relief       - Through the green.**
Taking the stance that would have been taken and using the club that would have been used, if the problem area had not existed, the player should swing the club, and determine the nearest point, (no nearer the hole and not in a hazard or on a putting green), from where a ball could be struck without interference to swing or stance by the problem area. The point where the ball would lie in that swing, is the nearest point of relief, and the one club length measurement can be measured from that point with any club; usually the driver. - **Wrong green** - same as "through the green", excepting, stance is not required to be off the green.

**Measuring Relief Dropping Area** - One and two club length drops can be measured with the club of choice. One club length measures are from the "nearest point of relief"; two club lengths measures from the problem point itself.

**When to Re-Drop.** Re-dropping is required if the dropped ball

  (1) comes to rest more than 2 club lengths from where dropped
  (2) comes to rest nearer the hole than the point of relief or problem point
  (3) rolls back inside the area from which relief is being taken (other than in the case of "unplayable ball" drops where this misfortune must be accepted)
  (4) rolls onto a green or into or out of a hazard
  (5) rolls out of bounds
  (6) strikes a player or players' equipment
  (7) was incorrectly dropped or dropped in a wrong place

If after re-dropping, proper relief has not resulted, (i.e. any of (1) to (5) above apply) the ball must be placed where the second drop landed. This is not the case where (6) or (7) applies, in which case, the ball is again re-dropped.

When dropping in a declared "dropping zone" the ball may roll outside the designated area; up to 2 club lengths from where striking the ground.

---

**G.U.R and Immovable Obstructions.** When dropping from G.U.R. or an immovable obstruction, a legal drop must result in the players stance being fully outside the G.U.R. or obstruction. No such requirement exists for dropping from **Hazards;** in which case re-dropping to ensure stance is clear of the hazard would incur a 2 stroke penalty and possible disqualification (see page 16 - ball played from wrong spot).

---

**Markers (Scorer) Consent.** All drops should be made with consent of the marker. If the marker does not believe that free relief is available, then the original ball should be played as lies and a second ball (nominated as the preferred ball) dropped and also played, for later decision by the committee. **21**

A ball can be declared unplayable anywhere on the course excepting when in a water hazard
- penalty one stroke.

To do so provides the following options:

## Through the green (fairway & rough)

(1) drop within two club lengths of where ball rests (not nearer the hole).
    For relief from large trees or bush areas this may not provide adequate relief.

(2) drop behind where the ball rests (no limit on distance) keeping that point between the drop point and the flag.

(3) play from place of previous shot.

If option (1) is taken but the drop does not result in full relief, a free re-drop is not permitted. This is the case even should the ball return to its original unplayable position.

## Bunkers

Same as above excepting under options (1) and (2), the ball must be dropped in the bunker.

# LOOSE IMPEDIMENTS

Loose impediments are natural objects that are not fixed and not growing. They include:
- dung
- grass clippings (not piled for removal), leaves & branches
- dead birds & animals
- rocks and stones
- worms and insects (and their mounds)

Loose impediments can be removed without penalty (excepting from hazards)

Loose impediments must be "loose" not solidly embedded and not adhering to the ball. Rocks can be loose impediments and help to remove them is permitted if done without undue delay. Leaves etc. stuck to a ball can only be removed on the green or when cleaning the ball in relief situations.

Sand and soil are loose impediments only on the putting green.

Snow and natural ice are both loose impediments and casual water at the players option.

Frost and dew are not loose impediments and they provide no relief.

If, through the green, a ball rolls as a result of removing a loose impediment a 1 stroke penalty results and the ball must be replaced. On the green - no penalty. **23**

These are artificial obstructions not easily moved, such as:
- internal fencing, sheds
- roads and paths (containing artificial materials)
- sprinkler heads, taps (faucets)
- stakes not easily moved (internal only - not O.O.B.)

**Ball in, on, or swing or normal stance interfered by.**
**Relief** - Where a ball is in:
(1) A water hazard - no free relief available.
(2) Any other part of the course - free relief - excepting, that:
   (i) Where it is clearly unreasonable to play a stroke because of some other factor such as a tree or roots, or
   (ii) The obstruction only interferes as a result of taking an abnormal stance, swing or direction of play, then .... free relief is not available.

The "where are you" pages record the manner in which relief is to be taken.

On the green, relief is also available from an obstruction on the line of putt.

Stakes (other than o.o.b. stakes) can be movable or immovable depending on how solidly embedded. Many clubs declare stakes to be immovable by local rule.

Paths and tracks of natural materials (dirt/clay) are not obstructions and no relief is available.

When taking relief, stance must be clear of the obstruction.

When a ball is lost in an immovable obstruction (other than in a water hazard) no penalty results and normal relief applies - relief is from estimated last entry point.

No relief is available for "line of sight". One club length from nearest point of physical relief is all that is available. Line of sight is only available where provided by local rule.

Movable obstructions are similar to loose impediments in that they are easily movable, the principal difference being that loose impediments are natural and movable obstructions artificial. Movable obstructions include:

- bottles and cans
- hoses
- ice (manufactured)
- planks
* - stakes - easily moved (internal only - not out of bounds)
- tools

    * Unless declared immovable by local rule

Movable obstructions can be removed, anywhere on the course.

Movable obstructions provide 2 advantages over loose impediments. They can be removed from hazards - loose impediments cannot, and secondly, if a ball moves as a result of removing an obstruction no penalty is incurred. With loose impediments immunity is granted only on the green.

A ball resting on or in a movable obstruction should be lifted, the obstruction removed, and the ball dropped (or on a green placed) as near as possible to its original position.

When a ball is lost in a movable obstruction no penalty results, and a ball is dropped, (or on the green placed) at the nearest possible point below where the obstruction was last entered, not nearer the hole. **25**

| Loose Impediments | Movable Obstructions | Immovable Obstructions |
|---|---|---|
| Don't remove in hazards | Remove anywhere | Don't remove anywhere |
| Stones | Bottles | Shed |
| Leaves | Cans | Internal fence |
| Sticks, branches, pine cones | Rakes | Roads & paths with artificial surface |
| Insects | Car (if unlocked) | Car (if locked) |
| Dead animals | Hoses | Taps |

The player is responsible for the accuracy of the score recorded for each hole on any lodged card, and for ensuring that both the player and marker have signed the card.

Should a score for any hole be recorded as less than what was actually taken the player is disqualified. Should a score for any hole be recorded as more than what was taken the player is not disqualified but the higher score stands. Failure by the player to sign the card results in disqualification.

Errors of addition or in applying the handicap shown on the card do not result in penalty. Responsibility for such lies with the committee.

**27**

*Golf courses in heaven are magnificent.*

*Bunkers are shallow, water can be walked on, and the greens are out of this world.*

*However, play is restricted to members only.*

*Good News! Membership lists are open, all welcome, and membership is free.*

*Register now and be sure of your place.*

*Apply to Secretary/Manager "Jesus" - before it's too late.*

May today be the day Lord!

28

## What does it mean?

Do unto others as you would have them do unto you.

Don't disturb or distract other players or in any way interfere with their right to play without harassment or intimidation.

Be safety conscious at all times; careful to never endanger others.

Be disciplined, courteous and sportsmanlike; not given to club throwing or other bad mannered or aggressive behaviour.

Be considerate of those following by allowing others to play through if your group is unable to keep up with those ahead.

Take care of the course, minimising damage wherever possible.

Repair divot holes you have made, pitch marks on greens and on completion of any hole any damage caused by golf shoes. Bunkers should be smoothed or raked after exiting. Care should be taken not to damage putting greens or putting green holes. Balls should not be removed from holes with club heads.

**Penalty for breach of acceptable etiquette standards.**

The committee may:
- for consistent disregard during a round or over a period of time, take disciplinary action including prohibiting an offender from course or competition play for a penalty period.
- for a serious breach, disqualify an offender

# DO I GET A DROP?

Can be purchased with your clubhouse, signature golf hole, or sponsor information on front and back cover.

(Minimum quantities apply)

Enquiries to ttdsa@bigpond.com

www.doigetadrop.com